**pay loader**

A noisy **bulldozer** moves in next to push the debris out of the way. Spinning, clattering tracks dig in and never get stuck!

The mighty **pay loader** scoops everything up and dumps it into waiting trucks.

bulldozer

**Earthmovers** are the biggest machines at the construction site. They crawl back and forth, pushing and pulling the rocks and dirt till the ground lies flat and even. Now the construction of the new building can begin!

dump truck

The powerful **track hoe** claws out a deep hole for the basement. Bucket loads of earth are scooped up and dropped into a waiting **dump truck**. When the truck is full, it rumbles off to dump its load, and another truck takes its place.

**track hoe**

The **cement truck** has a huge drum that spins around and around to keep its load soft and wet. When the cement is poured into the wooden forms, it dries to become the rock-hard foundation of the new building.

Workers unwind thick yellow cable from the **cable truck** and lay it in the ditches dug by the **backhoe**. Pipes for water and sewage are also lowered into place. Then the dirt is pushed back into the ditches to keep everything safe underground.

**cable truck**

backhoe

All day long the construction
site bustles with activity.
Machines and their operators
are hard at work. But one
machine brings everything to
a stop. With a blast of its horn,
the **lunch truck** arrives with
drinks and hot food for the
hungry workers. Break time!

lunch truck

The **sky crane** stretches out its long arm and hoists the steel beams into place. When bolted tightly together, the beams form the skeleton of the new building.

A cargo of concrete blocks is unloaded by the **boom truck**. Now construction of the outside walls can begin.

sky crane

boom truck

The new building is taking shape, but there is still plenty of work to do. Electricians, painters, roofers and many other tradespeople are busy inside and outside the building. The **forklift** delivers building materials wherever they're needed.

The building is finished
and the community center
is ready to open. The big
trucks and heavy machines
that helped to build it have
moved on to a new job.
The last truck at the site
is the **tree spade**.

Watch out, the next
construction site may be
right down your street!

**To Dane and Noah**

Text and illustrations © 2003 Don Kilby

Kids Can Press acknowledges the financial support of the Government of Ontario, through the Ontario Media Development Corporation's Ontario Book Initiative; the Ontario Arts Council; the Canada Council for the Arts; and the Government of Canada, through the BPIDP, for our publishing activity.

Published in Canada by
Kids Can Press Ltd.
29 Birch Avenue
Toronto, ON  M4V 1E2

Published in the U.S. by
Kids Can Press Ltd.
2250 Military Road
Tonawanda, NY  14150

www.kidscanpress.com

The artwork in this book was rendered in acrylic
The text is set in Univers.

Edited by Debbie Rogosin
Designed by Marie Bartholomew
Printed and bound in China

The hardcover edition of this book is smyth sewn casebound.
The paperback edition of this book is limp sewn with a drawn-on cover.

CM 03  0 9 8 7 6 5 4 3 2 1
CM PA 06  0 9 8 7 6 5 4 3 2 1

**Library and Archives Canada Cataloguing in Publication**

Kilby, Don
At a construction site / by Don Kilby.

(Wheels at work)

ISBN-13: 978-1-55337-378-0 (bound)  ISBN-10: 1-55337-378-2 (bound)
ISBN-13: 978-1-55337-987-4 (pbk.)  ISBN-10: 1-55337-987-X (pbk.)

1. Trucks—Juvenile literature.  2. Construction equipment-Juvenile literature.
I. Title. II. Series.

TL230.15.K534 2003          j629.224          C2002-902784-5

Kids Can Press is a Corus™ Entertainment company